SLOW PUNCTURE

The poetry of Miles Burrows was discovered in 1966 when Tom Maschler, already an editor at Cape, heard him give a public reading in London. Cape published him. After that, Burrows continued his life in many walks, most of them medical. Having studied Greats at Oxford, he was determined to become an intellectual and learned to smoke black Russian cigarettes, reviewing occasionally for the *New Statesman*. He worked as a GP and then as a psychiatrist. He was briefly a trawlerman, then a doctor in the New Guinea Highlands, in the American Hospital for Hmong tribe refugees on the Thai-Laos border, in a Catholic mission Hospital in Eastern Taiwan, in the Middle East and in Suffolk.

SLOW PUNCTURE

MILES BURROWS

CARCANET POETRY

First published in Great Britain in 2025 by
Carcanet
Main Library, The University of Manchester
Oxford Road, Manchester, M13 9PP
www.carcanet.co.uk

A CIP catalogue record for this book is
available from the British Library.

ISBN 978 1 80017 515 0

Book design by Andrew Latimer, Carcanet
Typesetting by LiteBook Prepress Services
Printed in Great Britain by SRP Ltd, Exeter, Devon

FSC
MIX
Paper | Supporting
responsible forestry
FSC® C014540
www.fsc.org

The publisher acknowledges financial
assistance from Arts Council England.

Supported using public funding by
ARTS COUNCIL
ENGLAND

CONTENTS

To Michael Schmidt and Su Fang for
salvaging an old bike

Faber must know.
A table to themselves in Waterstones.
(Once Faber *'and Faber'*
They started life as a *Doppelganger.)*
Their books spread over the table
Like a buffet.
They know about love and how to deal with it.
Familiar with shipwrecks, fogs,
Oceanography. *Nebelstreifs*
From one end to the other.

Meanwhile, back in the car, the forecast:
Fair Isle, Faroes, Cromarty, Forth:
Misty and murky through the morning.
For many of us looking forward to the Oval
It's going to be Put your wellies on this afternoon
Or sit in the car, to be honest, with your sandwiches.

AT BLAGNINI'S

As though love was a kind of fieldwork
In primitive exotic terrain
For which one had not prepared
By reading the recommended literature,
But which had to be written up
As if you had planned the whole thing in advance
To solve certain ill-definable problems,
And needed some original insight to present, looking back,
Like a general running after his troops
And writing a memoir of some disorganised
Smoke ridden skirmish:
– (Half the troops were not sure which side they were on
And one of them only joined to get time
To read a book under a hedge) –
Or as we need a story:
The purpose had to be invented afterwards.

DANCING WITH A CHAIR

> *'In old age he took dancing lessons, influenced by*
> *the philosophy of his friend Dr Mitzkin.'*

In old age, he took tango lessons,
Moving from Ross Street to Pretoria Road
Where women melting in a trance
Became supple as young girls.
Upstairs in Zion Baptist Hall
It's 'Keep your shoulders down.
As if wading up to the knees in sand.
And squashing a balloon
Between two chests. Never lose contact.
Lean forward from the ankles. Bottom in.
Then straight ahead. (It's Piazzola). Chin back.
Look after her. Be unpredictable.'
Dance there upon the shore. And later make
Expansive gestures to an empty room.

AT THE FLORIST'S

As a poet, you can get a job in a florist's.
Moyses Stevens
On Hay Hill, if you are in that part of London,
Though parking is difficult. Green Park
On the Picadilly Line. Little birds' nests
With a couple of wood anemones in moss
Sprinkled with morning dew that glistens
And a real mist. You meet interesting people
And in summer you can pull down a striped awning.
You have your spray and your can. Don't get drawn
Into polishing leaves. Across the road
There's a coffee shop
So you can mingle with students and artists.
Have a copy of *Zuricher Tagblatt*
Which you can't read. This can be helpful
In inducing a trance-like state
Called negative capability.
If you don't know any threatened flowers, refer to
Fisher's Chapter: 'Hangers on, Casuals and Fugitives.'

AUDIT

The sonnets lacked clarity
In a man of parts, a man of ability.
Turning tables for spirit rapping
They went before me like a blind man tapping.
Thoughts were organized in bright platoons
And bedded down in garrisoned emplacements
And marshalled at each point by strict dragoons
While eager virgins wept at gothic casements.

And the voice of God
Being hard to pick up without trembling
It's left on the plate like petits pois.
I must get home,
Away from Monica Metronome.

When I was young, I liked to say my prayers.
Already well cocooned in preference shares.
I lost my religion at the tote
And critics have me by the throat.

Standard Variations:
Two anaesthetists marched off in different directions
Each holding a loaded syringe.
Blue was the colour for the patient's drapes.
I was left holding in mid-air the final corner
Of the tiered canopy enveloping the patient.

If a poem is small enough
You could mistake it for a comma.
Control yourself sir, easy. Settle down.

PULL ME TOWARDS YOU, DARIMA

Play with my sandwich.
Lead my foot like a sliding door.
Do rapid unexpected things
Unlock my knees
Forget my feet.
Keep doing this but each time crossing over.
With go-come rocking movements.
Gather me in. Don't leave your body behind.
Stay by the fish and chip van
And Ben will tell me 'You are a cool cat'
And Mike will say 'You got it tonight'.

HORSES OF THE NIGHT

'O lente lente currite, noctis equi!'

Dear Mr D,
Grumbling that you are wounded by a woman's glance
Is a thing that poets do. I appreciate that.
The Horses of the Night
Are ridden by teenage girls in jockey caps
Bobbing up and down correctly with straight backs
As they trot along Barrington Road.

FOR DEATH, PRESS ONE

For death, press one.
For all other enquiries, please hold.
Thank you for calling death.
You have the option to hold (1), or let go (2).
Thank you for holding. My name is Frannie. Short for Francine.
Please be patient with us at this difficult time.
On a scale of 1–5 please grade your difficulty.
If you are calling about a loved one, press 1.
If it is about someone you feel a social obligation towards, press 2.
If it's about someone you wish you had loved but now it's too late, press 4.
You have pressed 11.
11 is not an impatient form of 1. It is its own number.
It is like looking into a driving mirror.
If you are driving pull into a designated parking space.
If you have a smart phone and a film of a mourning chaffinch, press one.
Thank you. You have pressed mourning chaffinch.
My name is Francine.

LITTLE BLACK DRESS

I wake alone at two in the morning
And find my hand pinching the enchanted horn
With three fingers at the tip
As if extinguishing a furtive cigarette
While the other hand gestures incisively
Into pitch darkness.
I search for words to go with the gesture
But feel the gesture, which no one can see,
Is incisive enough.
'A cocktail party, Amanda. You have to circulate.'
I look over her shoulder
Into the darkness. 'Black is always
A difficult colour.
Impossible to match.'

MAJOLIPORE SAUCE

Felis has met
An Indian man
At Gunter's. A Fellow of Botty's,
He makes his own majolipore sauce
And is teachiung her the flute.
I purse my lips as if sucking a bitter fluid through a thin straw.
He wants to give me a shirt
Which is too big for me.
He is a professor of gymnastics.
They are always professors.
Thousands of wildebeests gallop across the famished plains of Namibia.
He is teaching her the flute.
What's wrong with Worcester sauce?

NOT TOO LATE

It's not too late to go on the stage
As a butler in Australia.
I'll refer it to the ethics committee.
When you danced
Men were rising up for you
Like all the corn stalks of Asia.
I went through life with the emotions of a drama critic.
You brushed your teeth like a flautist
Holding the brush in both hands
Negotiating a tricky passage in Hindemith.
Everyone's writing their memoirs
Except you. People I knew
Have all grown shorter over the decades
Like short stories that have been edited.

SLOW PUNCTURE

Our yoga teacher says
Each posture has a mood
Like music. Sometimes a song
Can make us want to dance,
Another time the same tune makes you sad.
Don't suck in air too quick.
But breathe out like a host
Who keeps his guest at the doorway
Reluctant to let him go.
Breathe out like a bike with a slow puncture.
Her words are like spring water.
After class I see her standing in the dark street,
Talking into her mobile. I offer her a lift home
In my confusion forgetting
I have no car,
And my bicycle has no light.

SHALL I COMPARE THEE?

Tax assessment blows away cherry blossom
And summer lets are all too short term.
Look twice, your 'tan' has disappeared
And even Myra has to give a discount
Once she's been round the block.
Sunscreen apart she's all too natural.
The sun shines out of your anatomy.
I've sketched your assets in permanent ink
Giving you full possession with *lux perpetua*
And sole occupancy of my real estate.
It's no good Mr Death brandishing his umbrella:
The blogosphere is undeletable, darling.

Young men's poems may be forgiven.
For the old, there is really no excuse.
I said – Beryl, we don't want any theatricals.
We stayed at the Grimpenhorn.
Close to the skilift.
At *Silvesterabend* Mr Beilick said I should wear a hat
And Uncle Ed
Did his impersonation of King Farouk.

I went to a Hungarian in Chester Mews
You know how some people hold on
Practising tango in the kitchen
But it's not the same without a partner.

POETRY WORKSHOP

A terrible banging of spoons on the far side of the moon.

DO THE DEAD

Do the dead… you know?
I mean not, obviously, like we might
But more subtly, like having the vapours
Or interpenetrating like sea frets
Or Yeats inhaling a Harvey Wallbanger.

FRESHMAN AT PORTER'S GATE

Don't be a *dilettante*.
Be promising. Presentable.
Self-contained as a drowned cathedral.
Maybe I'll choose philosophy or very ancient history.
A few fragments of yesterday's news
In an alphabet no one could read.
Philosophy comes nearest to the occult.
I'll be a hermit by a waterfall
While hosts of Midian pitch their tents

And Madame Arcati's calling for a slow curtain.
I feel like an urn of uncertain provenance
Being auctioned at Sotheby's.

MEANWHILE BACK AT THE BANK

Meanwhile, at the bank in the hotel,
Ruth (it says on her lapel)
Wore some flowery overall of rough texture
Like a Gretchen
To make us feel we were really in a kitchen.
And gave me a friendly glance
As if to mind my fingers in the flour. I might get a chance
To run them round the edge of a bowl of parkin mixture.

(She reminded me of that motherly Chief Inspector
Who felt and understood my pain
In the underground carpark
Explaining there was nothing he could do
For my Nissan Micra clamped in Baker Street.
He understood my problem.
As if Wordsworth had been condemned
To walk the earth for seven years in chains beneath Park Lane).

MRS TANAKA'S DAUGHTER

I think of her at six years of age:
She carries her young brother on her back.
She herds the geese and the turkey in the field.
The turkey, taller than Shao Mei
Advances furiously in the yard
Scarlet wattles engorged with purple rage
Its neck and wings outstretched.
Shao Mei hits it on the head with her bamboo
Not sideswiping
But with an exact vertical swoop
Hits the top of its head.
Stunned, the turkey falls to the ground.
Afterwards, it looks at Shao Mei with respect
And dies.
We often think of Mrs Tanaka's daughter
Small in stature,
A teenager, she walks home across the graveyard.
In the dusk. A punk on a bicycle
Snatches her satchel. She sprints after him,
Pulls it off and swings it into his face.
– If I'm to be robbed I need a real robber
In a black leather jacket on a Ducati
Not a schoolboy in an old sweater
With drainpipe trousers!
Orphans and foundlings sweeping the temple yard,
We often think of Mrs Tanaka's daughter
And would like to marry her. This is not permitted.
It would disturb the harmony of the eight directions
And would upset Mrs Tanaka.
We often think of Shao Mei as she was then
With her long black hair

Washing her hair in the river at dawn
With Vinolia shampoo
And the monk in his robes running between the trees
In the golden light.
Mrs Tanaka has gone back to her village.
How we miss her sharp tongue!
Shao Mei is a high-flying executive
With multinational organisations
Head hunted and cherry picked
With iPad and iPhone.
She rides a Ducati in a black leather jacket
And has gone to that country from which no traveller returns:
America.
And we are left here in the temple yard
Old men sweeping, or standing in *kibu dachi*.   (The rider's stance)

STRIKING THE RIGHT NOTE

I had my Greek Apocalypse, while my brother
Collected old Wisdens. The couch was strewn
With copies of *The Stage* and *Plays and Players*
Horse and Hound and *Yachting World*
Knockout and *Wizard*.
When someone comes to tea up the gravel path
Mum says: Quick! What shall we be *doing?*
I'll be reading Chekhov and 'arranging flowers'.
And Dad? He'll be 'just coming in from hunting'.
Taking his boots off in the hall.
You be 'playing the piano'
And suddenly break off as they arrive.

I got a book on how to improve my memory:
Did you pay attention to your childhood?
Your dog? Your mother?
World War Two? At the time?
'Pay no attention' was the prevalent strategy.
When they shouted 'Your Mother's a cunt!'
We did not turn our heads
But continued walking along Knighton Rise
Towards Miss Piper's kindergarten in Westminster Road
With our velvet collars and Fair Isle berets.
At the drinks do
Betty was being thrown through a half-open doorway.
I continued to explain to my host how
Milne's universe, (like that of De Sitter),
Contains no matter.

THE SINGING COMPETITION

We always guessed
Time would go faster on the moon.
It could hardly go slower.
But If I was sitting at a table on the moon
Waiting for a bowl of soup
Would it take longer to arrive?

(– Because the Devil exists, Sister Catharine said,
Looking at me provocatively over a bowl of Betty Crocker
    cake mix.)
It would depend.
I mean if *time* was faster?
Or he could change his mind and have a sandwich.
Or a packet of crisps.

We always felt the moon had that look.
The way it kind of glides through the clouds
And hides its hands holding a pack of cards behind its back
Smiling in that way.
But if we are playing *mah-jong* we'll have less time to move.
By any standards.
Let us park that thought for a moment.

Time is not a waiter being rushed off his feet.
It could hang heavy.
German *lieder* would be going slower,
Before they got to the climax – (almost out of reach for the
    tenor who is trying not to raise his eyebrows) –
– *So manche Nacht*
In a–a–a–a–a–alter Zeit

And the accompanist wonders about his piano
And leans forwards a little with a straight back, towards the
   keyboard, listening.
And the judge, not knowing German, thinks:
– Is this the new music?

UNDER THE TREE

– Old ladies do *tai chi* from seven till eight a.m.
Old gentlemen drink herbal wine,
Gambling under the tree. They have a good time.
Karaoke. Order noodles. Lunch. Siesta.
And back to your tree. In the shade, out of the sun.
In the other corner: Filipinas with mobiles.
Old people in wheelchairs.
Indonesians. A Thai girl. They push them all under the tree.
The girls are giggling on their mobiles.
We can't blame the girls.
They push the old people into a corner.
We can't blame the Thai girls for this.

Old people can have a nap under the tree.
Yes, I love to see that. Indonesians. A Thai girl.
They push the old people all under a tree.
I mean don't blame the girls.
They push them all under the tree.

We can't blame the girls. They can watch the girls.

Mum was not allowed cats.
Sitting alone in a hotel lounge waiting for the bar to open.
With a man coughing his life out in the corner.
A small Tibetan nurse creeps up from behind
Puts her hands over Mum's eyes
And says: Guess Who?

When Mum had not very long to go
I was lying under the gate legged table in the hall,
On the Turkish rug
Reading Elizabeth David's
French provincial cookery for the second time,
Enjoying the word *bouillabaisse*
Mum was curled up by the telephone,
In her den, like a retired sea captain
Looking back over the Thames estuary
And could see through the knocked-through rooms of three cottages
Into the hall where I lay,
And through the dining room
Into the kitchen where the Consultus lady
Was staring out of the window
Dreaming of Kenya.
I knew Mum had hidden the Glenmorangie inside the Bendix.

PAPA'S LAST DAYS

He talked of his ashes being buried in Szechuan
In the village where he went fishing as a boy.
(Father Alaric's eyes brim with tears.)
He wants to give his money to people in that village.

I know something happened in that village
I told him he should buy you a jeep. We have to do that.
Glenfiddich and hot water, two Distalgesics
And a Mogadon, he should be out like a light.

He takes the Zimmer up the two steps to the bougainvillea tubs
He wants to buy you half a jeep.
He shouldn't.
You tell him.
He says he's over 70 and can't use the money.
Soaking the feet in potassium permanganate.

LOST OVERCOATS

The mind, sir, is a small town like Luton
Full of tiny apartments originally designed for something else,
The Foreign Office, like St Pancras Station
Still waiting for its diplomatic staff,
Its armies of *chinovniks* with lost overcoats
Its insoluble diplomatic contortions.

It is ready to hang linoleum over the moon, sir,
In beige stripes with a Greek key pattern
And will do so, come what may sir, come what may.

SONG FOR MAYDAY

A boy with broad shoulders.
In his head are nails and blue landscapes.
He comes when least expected, wearing his world like a sheath.
The stars are caught safely.
Turning her head to the left, she says we should just be friends.
She pares her love like a manicurist clearing out her fridge.
In the old wardrobe: sea voyages, a mental nurse.
Under the lawn, dragonflies are hatching.
'I admire Corinna, she drowned the kittens herself. She's so active,'
When you have toothache, flowers and candles are no help.
She is a figure on a Japanese screen.
It is time for the crowds to get off the lawn.
Behind the screen: a boy changing,
A woman combing out her red hair.
When she smiles, a bell is tolling in a college that is calling in the landscapes.
– Academics are messy eaters, she thinks.
Her smile is contented. Toothache is banished for the moment.
Her body flows with tears for her mother's death.

Corinna takes the kittens. They are warm in her arms, playing.
Where do bees get honey from in winter?
'They get it from wreaths in the graveyard' says the beekeeper.
The bees' legs are heavy with pollen.
Half asleep, they drag it into the hive across the snow.

THE ROAD TO IRKUTSK

I see them from my window
Lurching towards Grantchester through the snow
In gangs like convicted criminals,
Bearded, in headgear of red and brown, with dogs,
Trudging towards Siberia, nihilists.
And after them, some paces behind,
Smiling, come their wives
Pulling infants in heavy sledges
Bending down attentively to their infants,
Like wives of doomed convicts in chain gangs, nihilist wives
Who have willingly chosen to march with their husbands
As far as Irkutsk.
While I watch from an upstairs window,
A thin-lipped Mrs Epanchin
Widow of a half-pay general
And above us, flying in a wide chevron
In the bruised unshaven sky
Wild geese.

THE UPRIGHT PIANO

The piano makes a faint noise
Like my aunt's Jack Russell used to make
Listening to the Pearl Fishers,
Or as a meadow brown folds its wings
To resemble a dead leaf.
The desire to speak is a poised vibration.
Sigh once in a controlled way.
I'll get it to take a bit of the *chaconne*
Gently but firmly
Like getting a bit into a horse's mouth
While it's standing on your foot.
A piano always knows when you're nervous:
White moths in the sunless dampers
Skitter wildly in their interrupted dreams.

FATHER AND SON

– The most important thing in life, said Dad
Sitting beside me in the open 3 litre Riley
In the garage, facing the back wall…
Like critics facing the backdrop to a modern play.
(The stirrup pump, the folding canoe)…
I waited. Was it going to be religion?
Romance? Both topics usually avoided
In favour of sport and infringements
Of yacht racing rules, (how to avoid gybing
When going anticlockwise round a half sunken buoy
On the port tack close to a windward competitor
Was a typical conundrum, to be solved
In committee with card table, charts, and tiny model boats)
Or else it was to do with tennis:
Whose point if the ball stuck in the racket handle
In the gap in the frame where it joins the round bit?
(Urgent opinion was sought by telephone).

I waited, looking out of the stationary vehicle
At the back wall of the garage
(The fire hose, the folding canoe)
'Is to get yourself a really good pair of shoes' he continued
(After a pause)
'Decent, broad fitting, with a good welt.
You can't do better than Loakes. Local family firm.
Cathy Loake. Radcliffe Road. Comes to the tennis club.
Puts a spring in your step. Affects your whole Outlook on life.
I'd go for brogues'
I played with the cigar lighter in the walnut dashboard.
– This is my boy, he would say later on the hunting field
As if putting forward an item of dubious provenance.

PEARL FISHING

What is it about upright pianos
That makes you feel they would be happier lying down?
The tuner says there's some life in it yet
Though…here he is silent and plays a few
Enigmatic bits. Like a car which has done 100,000 miles, this piano
Has done so many Rachmaninoffs
Been bogged down in Brahmses, picked itself up so often after so
   many clashes,
And every one of them has left its scar.
Moths scuttle around when the top is opened
And you look down into a pit. Some notes are silent
As people under interrogation. The harder you hit them
The more obstinate they are. Others, the white ones
Like snowdrifts on the way to Moscow waiting for armies to give up
Or winter to change.
It would all be so easy if I could hit the notes.
I have the feeling. For Fauré's elegy
Played by a child on a cello on a summer evening in the next house.

I read my poem. Lady Brigit asks
As if choosing a twinset in an unsatisfactory chain store
Have you got something *quite different* you could show us?
A man reads a poem about Guatemala.
But – What is the point? Asks Rosetti.
I mean what is the status of the 'I' here?
I always find this worrying.
But what of the People who *built* this pyramid in Guatemala?
We cannot be silent about them We must ask.
What of the Common People, the Working Men?
Lady Brigit keeps us in order.
Her poem is a model of good taste.
She reads it, then clenches her jaw as if expecting a blow.

SPLEEN

'I thought you'd like to see Dr Levi. He's a new man, quite young.
You know, when you get to our age... We're giving him his head.'
I'm back in bed:
Dr Levi, with compassionate dark eyes,
Like a man who sold me a Turkish carpet
Is feeling my armpits
As you might feel for your watch under a cushion,
Or some elusive memory,
Will not stop looking there till he finds it.
Now, like a customs officer, he feels something the size of a pea.
He seems impressed
'We'll have this biopsied and then very soon...'
('I'm not tiring you, am I?')
I trusted a man selling me Turkish carpets.
And Nussbaum is back from behind the curtain.
'I thought you'd like Dr Levi.
But meanwhile we're thinking about taking out your spleen.'
'My *SPLEEN*?'
'The only way to biopsy it is to open you up.
Once the surgeon gets his hands on your spleen,
(You know what surgeons are like).
He'll whip it out. There's nothing we could do,
Even if I stood in theatre and held onto his *arm*.'
'But I *need* my spleen!'
'Not really. What do you need it for?'
'It is an essential ingredient of the Romantic Poet.'

After quarrelling with Sophie
I sit in the garden room
Reading poems of the late T'ang.
I'd cut a decent figure, a man of taste
In my hooded Canadian bear-hunter's corduroy jacket,
Reading poems of the late T'ang.
Or the middle T'ang. Even perhaps the Ming.
These poets had been dismissed from the civil service:
The usual distinguished academic drunks
In rusticated isolation
Claiming they loved the countryside
In verse like a cup of tea from a many times re-used teabag.
They send their verses to the Board of Merited Advancement.
With hidden envy, they look out from under tall hats.
Clothes are hanging out to dry,
Empty sleeves waving like the ghosts of dead children.

COUNTERFACTUAL

There should have been kookaburras and dingoes,
Grandparents who'd discovered the Murray river
With slabs of cream on their noses, scratching between their toes
As they sat on the porch in short trousers.
There should have been upside-down stars
And a monitor lizard upsetting the coffee table.
There should have been prim gardens and Ned Kelly in the dunny
And bush surgeons happy to do their first transvaginal
In the kitchen and pronging the sheilas,
There should have been brumbies and jackaroos from Monto
Treating their horses to buckets of Fosters
Outside the saloon with blowflies and kookaburras.
There should have been brunch coats.

THE 'WINTERFEST DO'

(Previously Christmas Party) was tonight.
Dr X got the blue, midnight blue corduroys.
He could still fit in at the waist if he held his breath and stood on tiptoe.
Belinda was away. The belt was imitation patent leather
Outside, but torn in places to reveal pieces of cardboard.
A costume belt. And blue-black corduroy shirt.
It was best to look a bit sinister in a night club.
He ironed the blue-black shirt.
He takes the Ermano Ferri shoes out of their box
In the loft. Made from a special breed of wild buck
Shot only at certain weeks in the year
In the Dolomites
So they said at the market, and on the box.
And he is Dr X.
Dr X tries a disco movement
In front of the wardrobe mirror
Making sure the neighbour couldn't see through the velux
('Disco Diva'), he had once been called.

On the bus from the camp to the night club
In front next to Samantha the practice nurse.
Who asked him when his wife was coming back.

The Admin girls waved in long dresses.
Dr X wears ski hat and brown corduroy jacket
With fur lined hood, made for a Canadian trapper.
'Dancing tonight?' asks Carianne.

In a converted barn, with exposed beams,
Several parties were going on.
Abba, Macarena, Sexy thing, and Cheeky Boy.

The girls, especially Kim and Mel, knew the words to the songs
And the gestures, stretching one arm out,
And slowly raising it, putting two hands against the cheek.

The girls had halter-backs and fine shoulders.
Blaise, who had been a concern for everyone,
Was now happy, with breasts practically falling out
Of a tie-up-in-front dress, which did not embarrass her at all.

Bel's husband took a photo with his digital.
At supper Dr X bought two bottles of red.
Matt, a fellow locum, bought 3 bottles of champagne.
Harriet felt flu coming on and had to go to the toilet to be sick.
Bel's husband explained how he'd bought the camera on a website.

Dr X spent time dancing by himself.
They were the kind of dances you would do that.
Relaxation was the key. The chief pharmacist, (a Scotsman
Who had still not been dismissed
Despite the efforts of the practice manager),
Was pulling some imaginary hosepipe
High into the air from the recesses of his groin.
Ottoline (*'I'm little, but I can take a bit'*)
In halter-back with blonde hair in dreadlocks
Began to copy him. Caught in the strobe lighting
With its curiously forensic aspect
As if displaying a flurry of shuffled criminal mugshots
Were some highly attractive girls in bloom of first youth
(One or two even still had dental plates),
And many a 60-year-old man and woman. Charlie Bulstrode
(Senior partner who was trying to sack Dr X)
Was dancing opposite Briony Smallgarden
Who was moving her pelvis as if controlling
A trotting horse on a short lead in dressage.

Dr X sat at the table. The men were in a group together
Ottoline's husband (Jez) did not dance at all.
Mel's husband danced about once.
The men tended not to dance.
They talked about laying patios.
Are you all right, Doctor X? called Zoe Pickersgill
Who had recently had a baby and had her hair cut short
In the latest fashion. She had caught Dr X off guard
Examining the exposed brickwork of the barn
With an expression that appeared gloomy but
Was more an age-related collapse of facial contours.

Yes, he said. He was fond of Zoe
Because her father had had three heart attacks
But she never seemed to brood about this
But was always looking after her flock of assistants.
Dr X sat back and had some red wine.
Doreen's husband related their tour of the Loire Valley.
People were discreetly glancing at their watches.
Dr X tried to glance at people's watches.

Balloons were inflated into sausages.
Then released to fly to the roof
Screaming and wriggling as they collapsed
In their final moment on the ceiling.
Dr X tried to blow but hadn't the strength.
He nearly blew out his eardrums. He put it back on the table.

It had been an enjoyable night in its way,
As in previous years.
In the gentlemen's toilet (GUYS)
There were three girls near the urinals making up their faces.
Dr X threatened to call the police
And they ran out giggling.

AT THE LAMASERY

Bob came out from the workshop behind the house
Advising him to get a workshop.
Asked him if he felt he was going mad,
They painted the gate. Bob did the difficult parts.
Life takes hold of you, he said, having divorced two wives.
They were the colours left in the cans.
They went on painting. A few drops of blue dripped on the path.
Opposite was the road, the bank, the grassy fells, the sky.
One of the lamas was learning to ride a bicycle.

BALLCOCK

When she is repairing the ballcock
In the toilet in the loft conversion,
Intent and focussed on the intricate and correct screw
Which she has identified after studying the mechanism
And twisting the screwdriver just the right amount
Snug without shearing the plastic,
Intent on watching the drops
That flow as tears from a holy statue
Of the Virgin Mary in a short story about an Italian village,
He looks half sideways
And sees the eyes of his great grandfather
Chief constable of Dewsbury,
Who arrested a bank robber in mid Atlantic,
And knows he is guilty and can see through all his evasions.

CONSULTATION

– But I was dying. And he saved my life.
– That's not the point.
– The treatment worked. I would have died.
The cells were down to zero
– Where is the tissue diagnosis?
– Well … You see, Professor Pfundt thought…
I mean it wasn't obvious. He had to go back
And study the slides. And then Honeypuss,
(I mean Dr Chiddingfold…)

– It's Intravenous *Harpic*. In the States
You'd sue the balls off me. Mainlining *Draino*.
And you had steroids with it.
IMAGINATIVE, I admit.

FIRST DAY OF SPRING

Everyone is falling in love with each other
Except you.
The birds built their nests in February.
Copulation takes a few seconds.
You hardly notice preening in sparrows.
Singing deters predators.
Cuckoos have gone to Egypt.
Only you on your Suzuki
Trapped between large trucks
Cutting you off with no helmet.
It's 6:30.
Birds imagine it is going to rain.
Mullas call from their towers.
A few liquid tinny spitting noises.

In Japan, cranes dance on their screens
One of them alone in the rice paddy
Pacing about among root crops and stubble.
Soon it will be time for the garbage trucks
Playing '*A maiden's prayer*'.
Housewives are gathering today's litter
And Granny is checking that no secret treasures,
(Hidden daily in different waste bins),
Are being discarded by mistake.
A thimble of water is put before the household deity
With a hint she can't expect a can of pineapple juice.

CAVE PAINTING IN THE AUVERGNE

Doreen falls asleep in the car while
M Stompadou underground
Chews charcoal mixed with an astringent dye,
And spits the atrocious slime against the wall
In re-enactment of stone age art.
He spews staccato droplets through a straw
Pph-pp pf-pp pfpf pp p-p-p-p
Spluttering like an outboard motor
Or the stammering erotic cries of Monteverdi.
A bison is puked onto a tube train
While muscles round the artist's mouth
Contorted into spasms by the bitter dye
Convey an expression of extreme remorse.

Sunlight dazzling as migraine.
Black butterflies, prayers from the dead
Burnt fragments of unopened letters
Rise and fall in the heat.

CLEANING THE BATHROOM

He says he's going to clean the bathroom
But I know he is going to watch the Paris Open.
He's excited by two young women.
One, Konta, all in black like a poisonous spider
Leaping about like a black widow in sharp sunlight,
The other one hardly nineteen,
So calm, not out of breath
Eyes soft and quiet as if she is somewhere else
Leaning forwards slightly with a straight back
Adjusting a piano stool, about to play
Bach's Adagio in G.
He can't stop talking about her abstract face.
She loses. But not to him. Cleaning the bathroom.
He feels like an empty stadium.

CONDOLENCES

I was concerned to hear about your hamster, Beryl,
Being run over in the stadium.
It haunts me like reports
Of Caesar's reversals in Bithynia.
I missed my lunch.
It was going to be grilled whitebait.
And that little patch under the left eye.
Wasn't King Battus
Suckled by a hamster in the woods of Smyrna?
I'm sure he was well descended. He was erudite.
We could have taken him to a gerbil show.
The way he ran about like that
In the bed. My lips are sealed.
I'm thinking of a four- part mass in the manner of Albinoni.
I can't look at trams anymore.
But perhaps you could get a replacement?
After all, when Lucius was poisoned by that mushroom
You hardly had time for the morning after pill
Before teaming up with Marco.
How's his acting? Don't bring me more tears.

CONSULTATION FOLLOW-UP

Had I been cured by accident?
The only way to prove it was by getting a relapse.
My hair fell out. I was like a Greek statue.
In a week it grew back bushier.
At work, in the lift, a bald Pakistani porter points to my thick mane.
– Doctor! Your hair!

CROOKED ECLIPSES

And I should be headmaster on the moon
And master it in all its phases
And cut it down to size in trenchant phrases.

Headmastership! Or else a rural dean
Sitting with my chapter in a close,
Or playing croquet on a quiet green
I should be less morose.

ENTRY FOR MARCH

One day is enough at this stage. How about today?
Primroses out in force.
Good results from specialist.
Though it's probably cancer.
He said it's my choice.
'What would you choose?' He looked older than me
And much kinder.
He said he'd probably do nothing.
Surrender to the heart.
I run after it with a white flag through the wood.

FLY IN A BOTTLE

Talking to this woman
Why do I feel like a fly in a bottle?
An empty sherry bottle of Harvey's Bristol Cream
A fly should never have crawled into.
Inside: midsummer twilight. There should be a cork,
Or what tall ship will heave into the offing
As the windjammer *Passat*, last of the tall ships
Took Uncle Dennis from Dewsbury,
Tired of selling vacuum cleaners round Batley,
To work before the mast
Leaving nothing but a note on the kitchen table:
'*Gone to Sea*'?

FREQUENCES

Doreen is a very intelligent kind of woman,
You know the intelligent type
– Do you think I'm intelligent? She asks
– Yes, I say
And it's true. She's always, you know, checking things.
She checks the wastepaper baskets.
To read impressions made by ballpen on the other pages.
She can hear if I've not done up my zip.
It's tiring to be like that.
That's why she has to lie down.
She has to lie down to save power or blowing a fuse.

GATEWAY HOTEL (WHEN THE BLACKBIRD IS WHITE)

The Gateway Hotel had him on the spot.
(Gateway to where? he wondered. Gateway to what?)
– First, I must *ch ch ch* my eyebrows.
– *Ch ch ch?*
– Yes. Ch ch ch. Am I boring you?
– If I'm bored, I can always read my book.
It's about a bank robbery in Sweden.
– You know how to make the comedy about a crying girl?
People were selling balloons at the door of the church.
Posters of Jesus in a tarot pack,
The face repeated, a political candidate,
Serial photos of a patient who is not getting any better.
Fishermen with inner tubes round their waists
Are wading out with torches on their heads,
Waist deep till they tread water
With small candles burning on top of their heads
Like dead people crossing the great river.

LENDING

She lent herself to love
As a pavement after rain

LIFE CLASS

At Beppo's, in the break, the Spaniard
Is chatting to the Russian-Hungarian
About his pastels.
Jeanette
Has very well-fitting tailor-made jeans
And stands in unconscious *contraposto*.
Her straight brown-blonde hair hangs down
Sheer as a waterfall. She is wearing chocolate
Brown, with some embroidery on the cuffs.
The Spaniard is explaining how he would paint her in oil pastel
She is a technical problem.
She enjoys being treated as a technical problem.

I dreamt the Spaniard and Hungarian were really French,
They had been wearing
Baggy English clothes as a joke but now appeared
On the tennis court, the 'Spaniard' (French)
In brown patterned
Crisp designer tennis shorts with matching
Small waistcoat costing
Thousands spent casually. He had been wearing
Sloppy English clothes
Laughing when seeming to be part of us.
And his Hungarian (French) partner appeared
In a matching *cache sexe* at the front,
And some kind of waistcoat on the top
And the cute small round bottom
Bare, crisp and self-assured
White, pretty and shining
As an after-dinner coffee cup.

I had seen a picture
Of a pop singer with buttocks so small
They appeared compressed to the size of a thimble.
But this Hungarian (French) girl was wearing hers crisper,
Sharper, sunnier, almost as if
She was wearing a daffodil for cancer relief.
The Spaniard served for a knock up
So fast that the ball bounced right over the back safety netting.

IN HALLWAYS

Moon-dwellers say all lost objects
Are on the Earth, their true home.
They see, dotted over our planet
In spacious parkland, manor houses,
People who mislaid themselves beyond retrieval,
Who wait like umbrellas in hallways. They tap barometers
Pacing up and down like dogs
Waiting to be taken for a walk. Their nervous faces
Turn eagerly to any visitor in case
He may recognise them. Mum is there.
I lost her at the station. But no train is going.
No Blue Train. No Pullman sleeping car.
No passport control in the night.

My father died at exactly the right time.
Not because he suddenly put all the lights out
In the middle of his cocktail party
But like Drobny and the King of Sweden
In their long cream flannel trousers, who retire
Before they get too old, in their club sweaters,
Not hanging about on the flat roof of the tennis club.
Forlorn figures hoping to fill in for a foursome.

Some compare life with Russian billiards
But tennis comes to mind
With its sudden tides and inner dramas,
The way the umpire says Quiet Please!
And the special meaning for the word *Love*.

MEMNON

I told a woman in the post office it was a fine day.
She looked at me as if the giant statue of Memnon
Had suddenly uttered a cry at dawn in the desert.
I still have two legs that go nicely
And the brain comes along like an old dressing gown
You can't bring yourself to throw away.

I bought a book on how to improve your memory
Where did I put it?
The secret is to pay attention at the time.
Did you pay
Attention to your childhood?
Your dog? Your mother?
World War Two? At the time?
'Pay no attention' was the prevalent strategy.
When they shouted 'Your Mother's a cunt!'
We did not turn our heads
But continued walking along Knighton Rise
Towards Miss Piper's kindergarten in Westminster Road
With our velvet collars and Fair Isle berets.
At the drinks do
Betty was being thrown through a half open doorway.
I continued to get a book on how to improve my memory.
I try to explain to my host how
Milne's universe, (like that of De Sitter),
Contains no matter.

MISSING YOU

Did you know the moon was so old
It might have to go into a home?

It keeps edging nearer
The way old people do.

Goya wore candles on his hat
But Humphrey Davy invented the miners' lamp.

On Enceladus a day is longer than a year.
Tonight, we have the Spanish Civil War.

You can't go on like this, moon,
Peering into people's bedrooms
And the stars have their own lives to lead.
When did you last think of Cassiopea? Really? Think!
You must pull yourself together, moon.
You say you remember things
What can you remember?
It's embarrassing. You think you're all right.
Only yesterday you put rice crispies in the fridge.

What's going to happen next?
If your hand trembles, sit on it. Wipe your mouth.
Skittering about. When did you have a decent job?

Your voice is like a nervous cough.
You must pull yourself together
And shut the door if you can't sing in tune.

Your eyes look like two catacombs

And make me think of furnished rooms.

We've heard enough of Grandad's work in Leeds.
Your eyes look like abandoned creeds.

MUSIC ROOM

Cough between movements, never clap.
Bark is the best composer. Norris
Can play The Queen of Sheba with both hands
Though it's for two pianos. Clements
Can play the organ and wear mauve socks.
Those with aptitude go to Mr Draper.

A symphony has three movements
Count and know when to cough.
An oboe sounds like a duck.
D minor is the saddest chord.

PRESENT COMPANY EXCEPTED

This Anthology of Love Poetry.
What do they want?
After the dawn chorus, birds settle down.
They find a mate or build a nest on their own
Keep quiet till next morning.
And scuttle under a hedge.
My father used to chat with travelling Jehovah Witnesses
In the garage.
They played their scriptures on gramophone records
While he was mending the sails of his dinghy.
Poets always say the same thing. That's why we listen.
Some tiny fragment from Irish.

RAKEHELLS

We would be rakehells.
Our cigars would be rolled
On the thighs of young Cuban women.
Koebner already had a suede waistcoat.
In the afternoons we wandered the reed beds
By the mere, looking for the mummified phallus
Of a hyena, that Mr Malmstrom had read to us about
In a story by Dennis Wheatley.
We invoked Asmodeus, a satanic winged horse.
Malmstrom had left after a term
With Wheatley unfinished
And the man in the wheelchair still paralysed
As poisonous spiders marched towards him in military
   formation
Illuminated by a haggard shaft of moonlight.

REFLECTIONS

I saw my backside the other night
Pale and wrinkled, like an elderly great aunt
You haven't seen for decades
And suddenly meet on a train.

When she turns her head to the left
The bells are calling in the landscapes.

I checked everything with Patricia
She said she had 16 dog poets
And 8 cat poets
But no puppies.

Yesterday we learnt about Venus.
It's covered in basalt, rains all the time.
Mostly sulphuric acid.
Next week it's the Zoroastrians.

SONNET

When you left
To stay with your sister
In New Zealand
For an open-ended period,
To 'find out who you were'
You left your under-things in my drawer
Wrapped in their own plastic bag.

STRING THEORY

And you can't run love backwards
Even if you wanted to
It's a form of anxiety.
We can hardly remember
What it was like before the war.

TEARS

We can prescribe tears now. It's in the guidelines.
– Doctor, can you make me cry?
Tears represent a saving
For the National Health Service.
And may be found in the Formulary under 'Tears'
   a) Artificial (acrylic polymers)
   b) Tears 'Naturale' for private patients,
Salvaged from Egyptian tombs, already wept
By betrayed women, guilty widows, hysterics,
Now reused
By those who have none left to shed.
Distilled from brackish wetlands,
Autumn tears, the tears of spring.
Salt on your lips after a swim.

THE REUNION

'I'm worried: all the people
Will be more successful than me.'
'Oh don't worry. They're all complete failures.
You'll be shaking hands with one pillar of salt after another.'
'Pitt was Prime Minister at our age'
Peel had a smile like the silver plate on a coffin.
We could smile like that even if we could not be Prime
   Minister.
(And even if we could not be in the eighteenth century).
Our slang was referred to mists of antiquity
Though invented by Major Bradley in 1949.
The secret of getting up was not to wake up,
Advice that would last us through our working lives.
In Botticelli's *Primavera*
Mercury turned away
To poke the clouds with a stick.
The bright day had begun.

THE CONVENTIONAL VIEW

I dreamt a girl was sitting on my lap
Saying Come into me, and all that sort of thing
And I said No, proud of myself in my dream.
Should we be proud of ourselves in dreams?
That is the question I put to you this morning.
And her lying there saying
– I think you're alert to the conventional view of history.
I never expected that.
So she burst into tears and I held her hand.
When we lost Eden we moved on.
But when we lost that old tennis ball on Christmas Day
We kept looking for ages in the grass.

Everyone is falling in love
Except you.
The birds, well
Insemination takes a few seconds.
Preening is forever
It's 930. The birds are taking a break.
They imagine it is going to rain.
In Qatar mullahs call from towers.
While religious police check the barber shops.
The birds make a few gurgling sounds
A liquid tinny spitting noise
Like someone rinsing their mouth out at the dentist.

VILLA IN SPAIN

How many donkeys can you see in Draycott Gardens?
Spain is a magical country. But then so is Portugal.
It's an emotional country. They discovered Brazil.
In the Civil War they had to stop the bullfights.
Caroline's mother's plumber
Has a villa in Spain.
It's not that we feel we can't go there.
But somehow *Desencantado*.
Caroline do brighten up.

WHITE MARGINS

At the circumcision party
A large penis carved out of butter – (Mum was an art
    student) –
Decorated the table.
The bass notes of the rabbi in tall black hat
Console the tearful apple-cheeked women folk
Shut for a moment in the kitchen.

Dad would never sit down for long.
But if he did, would read Churchill's War Memoirs.
I smiled, wondering how he could read them again
When he could be reading *Angelique and the Sultan,*
Or the story about two French schoolboys
In a bathing hut, which Mum found
And I never saw again but remember the dust jacket.
Or he could have dipped into *The Eye of Horus*
Though he stuck with C of E
While I was hypnotised by the word Heidegger
And murmured it at parties with a bemused expression.
Dad was still reading The Eye of the Storm (and Jorrocks)
Now, already at the back end of life
I sit with a bar of bitter chocolate.

READING GLASSES

Too vain to wear glasses
We go on reading our favourite novel
In its red cloth binding
Like the colour of curtains faded in sunlight,
Or the cassock of some retired, perhaps discredited, missionary bishop,
Forgetting the plot which we knew once
And unable to make out the characters' names
'– *She wrapped her arm round me like a stole.*
It gave her a sense of reliability.
– A sense that was shattered when you made advances
To Mrs Vereagle.
– Advances?
– You were at her like a ferret in a sack sir.'
Unable to remember the plot or read the lines,
But remembering we loved the novel
From our favourite novelist,
We turn the well-loved pages under the lamplight
So that other characters
With names like Mrs Vershinin
Are always hovering in the wings
Despite the reading light over our shoulder
Like an approaching migraine.
We go on turning the pages
Revisiting a landscape, dazzled by the reading light
Making out vague forms
Strangely altered from faces we knew in childhood
And even changing as we look.
What good value these old novels are!
Who would dream they could be read upside down
And back to front
Like a landscape seen by a child hanging upside down in a tree?

UNCLE VANYA DRINKS HIS OWN POETRY

Auntie Biddy could never get the hang of poetry
And was so hopeless that she put other people off.
She was asked to sit outside the classroom and do knitting in the corridor,
Which she was happy to do,
But still peered in through the glass pane in the door.
– Poetry? What happened to woodwork?
You can do anything at 70 now.
My solicitor plays tennis with 2 knee replacements.
There are people jogging every morning beneath my window.
They stop when they get round the corner.
They stoop forward as if reaching out in longing for the further shore.
I tried jogging, and a woman said:
– I thought you were a *horse* coming up behind me.
All that puffing and blowing. Not doing you any good you know!
People write things on walls,
Critics are cleaning ladies with their smiles and buckets.
And used to have names like Harold Nicholson
Or Kenneth Clarke, and would tell us what we really liked.
'Glancing again at what we always feel
Must be an early student of Memlinck
In the little church of Santa Maria della Condolenza,
Who is not reminded of that remark by Berenson
That the back view of a woman is,
From the point of view of line and mass,
More satisfactory?'
And we think yes of course.
2 women in America are arrested for assaulting a traffic policeman.
(A long loving shot as they are being driven to the courthouse in
    handcuffs).
This is followed by a wild pony in Alaskan muskeg
That has fallen into a bog

And is waiting to die as its back legs and haunches are being sucked
    down.
It is pushing up with its front legs
As if trying to heave itself out
Immobile and very young. Big expressive eyes.
Suddenly there arrive two people with a lasso and a belt
Like a transmission belt which they manage to fit
Round the submerged back end of the pony,
And winch it out gently without breaking its legs.
The pony trots away, with just a brief nod
Like a poet rescued by a small magazine.

At school we were groomed to be well-informed.
The Connoisseur taught us what furniture to appreciate,
What country estates in Radnorshire to acquire.
At least we could become housekeepers,
Agents, or auctioneers.
The kind of people who hold up objects at Christie's
Or lie against the bonnets of slim cars.
We were all spinning round in The *Wheel of Fire*
Like a cake mix. New York poets.
Stefan was a lecturer in Fashion.
He wrote a poem that began
'The full moon, like an aspirin caught in the throat of a hysterical
    woman...'